ADMIRABILE SIGNUM

ADMIRABILE SIGNUM

Apostolic Letter
of the Holy Father
Francis

on the Meaning and Importance
of the Nativity Scene

VERITAS

Published 2022 by
Veritas Publications
7–8 Lower Abbey Street
Dublin 1
Ireland
publications@veritas.ie
www.veritas.ie

ISBN 978 1 84730 963 1

10 9 8 7 6 5 4 3 2 1

A catalogue record for this book is available from the British Library.

Designed by Veritas Publications
Images: cover, p. 5, p. 8, p. 16 and p. 20 © mammuth/istockphoto.com;
p. 12 © GoodGnom/istockphoto.com.
Printed in the Republic of Ireland by Walsh Colour Print, Kerry

Veritas Publications is a member of Publishing Ireland.

*Veritas books are printed on paper made from the wood pulp of managed
forests. For every tree felled, at least one tree is planted, thereby renewing
natural resources.*

1. The enchanting image of the Christmas crèche [crib], so dear to the Christian people, never ceases to arouse amazement and wonder. The depiction of Jesus' birth is itself a simple and joyful proclamation of the mystery of the Incarnation of the Son of God. The nativity scene is like a living Gospel rising up from the pages of sacred Scripture. As we contemplate the Christmas story, we are invited to set out on a spiritual journey, drawn by the humility of the God who became man in order to encounter every man and woman. We come to realise that so great is his love for us that he became one of us, so that we in turn might become one with him.

With this Letter, I wish to encourage the beautiful family tradition of preparing the nativity scene in the days before Christmas, but also the custom of setting it up in the workplace, in schools, hospitals, prisons and town squares. Great imagination and creativity is always shown in employing the most diverse materials to create small masterpieces of beauty. As children, we learn from our parents and grandparents to carry on this joyful tradition, which encapsulates a wealth of popular piety. It is my hope that this custom will never be lost and that, wherever it has fallen into disuse, it can be rediscovered and revived.

2. The origin of the Christmas crèche is found above all in certain details of Jesus' birth in Bethlehem, as related in the Gospels. The evangelist Luke says simply that Mary 'gave birth to her firstborn son and wrapped him

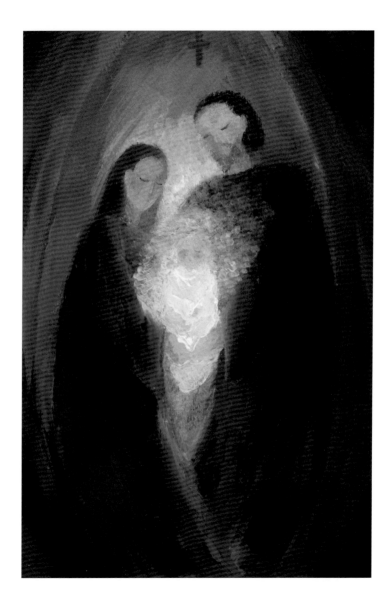

in swaddling cloths, and laid him in a manger, because there was no place for them in the inn' (2:7). Because Jesus was laid in a manger, the nativity scene is known in Italian as a *presepe*, from the Latin word *praesepium*, meaning 'manger'.

Coming into this world, the Son of God was laid in the place where animals feed. Hay became the first bed of the One who would reveal himself as 'the bread come down from heaven' (Jn 6:41).

Saint Augustine, with other Church Fathers, was impressed by this symbolism: 'Laid in a manger, he became our food' (Sermon 189, 4). Indeed, the nativity scene evokes a number of the mysteries of Jesus' life and brings them close to our own daily lives.

But let us go back to the origins of the Christmas crèche so familiar to us. We need to imagine ourselves in the little Italian town of Greccio, near Rieti. Saint Francis stopped there, most likely on his way back from Rome where on 29 November 1223 he had received the confirmation of his Rule from Pope Honorius III. Francis had earlier visited the Holy Land, and the caves in Greccio reminded him of the countryside of Bethlehem. It may also be that the 'Poor Man of Assisi' had been struck by the mosaics in the Roman Basilica of Saint Mary Major depicting the birth of Jesus, close to the place where, according to an ancient tradition, the wooden panels of the manger are preserved.

The Franciscan Sources describe in detail what then took place in Greccio. Fifteen days before Christmas,

Francis asked a local man named John to help him realise his desire 'to bring to life the memory of that babe born in Bethlehem, to see as much as possible with my own bodily eyes the discomfort of his infant needs, how he lay in a manger, and how, with an ox and an ass standing by, he was laid upon a bed of hay'.[1] At this, his faithful friend went immediately to prepare all that the Saint had asked. On 25 December, friars came to Greccio from various parts, together with people from the farmsteads in the area, who brought flowers and torches to light up that holy night. When Francis arrived, he found a manger full of hay, an ox and a donkey. All those present experienced a new and indescribable joy in the presence of the Christmas scene. The priest then solemnly celebrated the Eucharist over the manger, showing the bond between the Incarnation of the Son of God and the Eucharist. At Greccio there were no statues; the nativity scene was enacted and experienced by all who were present.[2]

This is how our tradition began: with everyone gathered in joy around the cave, with no distance between the original event and those sharing in its mystery.

Thomas of Celano, the first biographer of Saint Francis, notes that this simple and moving scene was accompanied by the gift of a marvellous vision: one of those present saw the Baby Jesus himself lying in the manger. From the nativity scene of that Christmas in 1223, 'everyone went home with joy'.[3]

3. With the simplicity of that sign, Saint Francis carried out a great work of evangelisation. His teaching touched the hearts of Christians and continues today to offer a simple yet authentic means of portraying the beauty of our faith. Indeed, the place where this first nativity scene was enacted expresses and evokes these sentiments. Greccio has become a refuge for the soul, a mountain fastness wrapped in silence.

Why does the Christmas crèche arouse such wonder and move us so deeply? First, because it shows God's tender love: the Creator of the universe lowered himself to take up our littleness. The gift of life, in all its mystery, becomes all the more wondrous as we realise that the Son of Mary is the source and sustenance of all life. In Jesus, the Father has given us a brother who comes to seek us out whenever we are confused or lost, a loyal friend ever at our side. He gave us his Son who forgives us and frees us from our sins.

Setting up the Christmas crèche in our homes helps us to relive the history of what took place in Bethlehem. Naturally, the Gospels remain our source for understanding and reflecting on that event. At the same time, its portrayal in the crèche helps us to imagine the scene. It touches our hearts and makes us enter into salvation history as contemporaries of an event that is living and real in a broad gamut of historical and cultural contexts.

In a particular way, from the time of its Franciscan origins, the nativity scene has invited us to 'feel' and

'touch' the poverty that God's Son took upon himself in the Incarnation. Implicitly, it summons us to follow him along the path of humility, poverty and self-denial that leads from the manger of Bethlehem to the cross. It asks us to meet him and serve him by showing mercy to those of our brothers and sisters in greatest need (cf. Mt 25:31-46).

4. I would like now to reflect on the various elements of the nativity scene in order to appreciate their deeper meaning. First, there is the background of a starry sky wrapped in the darkness and silence of night. We represent this not only out of fidelity to the Gospel accounts, but also for its symbolic value. We can think of all those times in our lives when we have experienced the darkness of night. Yet even then, God does not abandon us, but is there to answer our crucial questions about the meaning of life. Who am I? Where do I come from? Why was I born at this time in history? Why do I love? Why do I suffer? Why will I die? It was to answer these questions that God became man. His closeness brings light where there is darkness and shows the way to those dwelling in the shadow of suffering (cf. Lk 1:79).

The landscapes that are part of the nativity scene also deserve some mention. Frequently they include the ruins of ancient houses or buildings, which in some instances replace the cave of Bethlehem and become a home for the Holy Family. These ruins appear to be inspired by the thirteenth-century Golden Legend of the Dominican Jacobus de Varagine, which relates a pagan belief that the Temple of Peace in Rome would collapse when a Virgin gave birth. More than anything, the ruins are the visible sign of fallen humanity, of everything that inevitably falls into ruin, decays and disappoints. This scenic setting tells us that Jesus is newness in the midst of an aging world, that he has come to heal and rebuild, to restore the world and our lives to their original splendour.

5. With what emotion should we arrange the mountains, streams, sheep and shepherds in the nativity scene! As we do so, we are reminded that, as the prophets had foretold, all creation rejoices in the coming of the Messiah. The angels and the guiding star are a sign that we too are called to set out for the cave and to worship the Lord.

'Let us go over to Bethlehem and see this thing that has happened, which the Lord has made known to us' (Lk 2:15). So the shepherds tell one another after the proclamation of the angels. A beautiful lesson emerges from these simple words. Unlike so many other people, busy about many things, the shepherds become the first to see the most essential thing of all: the gift of salvation. It is the humble and the poor who greet the event of the Incarnation. The shepherds respond to God who comes to meet us in the Infant Jesus by setting out to meet him with love, gratitude and awe. Thanks to Jesus, this encounter between God and his children gives birth to our religion and accounts for its unique beauty, so wonderfully evident in the nativity scene.

6. It is customary to add many symbolic figures to our nativity scenes. First, there are the beggars and the others who know only the wealth of the heart. They too have every right to draw near to the Infant Jesus; no one can evict them or send them away from a crib so makeshift that the poor seem entirely at home. Indeed, the poor are a privileged part of this mystery; often they are the first to recognise God's presence in our midst.

The presence of the poor and the lowly in the nativity scene remind us that God became man for the sake of those who feel most in need of his love and who ask him to draw near to them. Jesus, 'gentle and humble in heart' (Mt 11:29), was born in poverty and led a simple life in order to teach us to recognise what is essential and to act accordingly. The nativity scene clearly teaches that we cannot let ourselves be fooled by wealth and fleeting promises of happiness. We see Herod's palace in the background, closed and deaf to the tidings of joy. By being born in a manger, God himself launches the only true revolution that can give hope and dignity to the disinherited and the outcast: the revolution of love, the revolution of tenderness. From the manger, Jesus proclaims, in a meek yet powerful way, the need for sharing with the poor as the path to a more human and fraternal world in which no one is excluded or marginalised.

Children – but adults too! – often love to add to the nativity scene other figures that have no apparent connection with the Gospel accounts. Yet, each in its own way, these fanciful additions show that in the new world inaugurated by Jesus there is room for whatever is truly human and for all God's creatures. From the shepherd to the blacksmith, from the baker to the musicians, from the women carrying jugs of water to the children at play: all this speaks of the everyday holiness, the joy of doing ordinary things in an extraordinary way, born whenever Jesus shares his divine life with us.

7. Gradually, we come to the cave, where we find the figures of Mary and Joseph. Mary is a mother who contemplates her child and shows him to every visitor. The figure of Mary makes us reflect on the great mystery that surrounded this young woman when God knocked on the door of her immaculate heart. Mary responded in complete obedience to the message of the angel who asked her to become the Mother of God. Her words, 'Behold I am the handmaid of the Lord; let it be to me according to your word' (Lk 1:38), show all of us how to abandon ourselves in faith to God's will. By her 'fiat', Mary became the mother of God's Son, not losing but, thanks to him, consecrating her virginity. In her, we see the Mother of God who does not keep her Son only to herself, but invites everyone to obey his word and to put it into practice (cf. Jn 2:5).

At Mary's side, shown protecting the Child and his Mother, stands Saint Joseph. He is usually depicted with staff in hand, or holding up a lamp. Saint Joseph plays an important role in the life of Jesus and Mary. He is the guardian who tirelessly protects his family. When God warned him of Herod's threat, he did not hesitate to set out and flee to Egypt (cf. Mt 2:13-15). And once the danger had passed, he brought the family back to Nazareth, where he was to be the first teacher of Jesus as a boy and then as a young man. Joseph treasured in his heart the great mystery surrounding Jesus and Mary his spouse; as a just man, he entrusted himself always to God's will, and put it into practice.

8. When, at Christmas, we place the statue of the Infant Jesus in the manger, the nativity scene suddenly comes alive. God appears as a child, for us to take into our arms. Beneath weakness and frailty, he conceals his power that creates and transforms all things. It seems impossible, yet it is true: in Jesus, God was a child, and in this way he wished to reveal the greatness of his love: by smiling and opening his arms to all.

The birth of a child awakens joy and wonder; it sets before us the great mystery of life. Seeing the bright eyes of a young couple gazing at their newborn child, we can understand the feelings of Mary and Joseph who, as they looked at the Infant Jesus, sensed God's presence in their lives.

'Life was made manifest' (1 Jn 1:2). In these words, the Apostle John sums up the mystery of the Incarnation. The crèche allows us to see and touch this unique and unparalleled event that changed the course of history, so that time would thereafter be reckoned either before or after the birth of Christ.

God's ways are astonishing, for it seems impossible that he should forsake his glory to become a man like us. To our astonishment, we see God acting exactly as we do: he sleeps, takes milk from his mother, cries and plays like every other child! As always, God baffles us. He is unpredictable, constantly doing what we least expect. The nativity scene shows God as he came into our world, but it also makes us reflect on how our life is part of God's own life. It invites us to become his disciples if we want to attain ultimate meaning in life.

9. As the feast of Epiphany approaches, we place the statues of the Three Kings in the Christmas crèche. Observing the star, those wise men from the East set out for Bethlehem, in order to find Jesus and to offer him their gifts of gold, frankincense and myrrh. These costly gifts have an allegorical meaning: gold honours Jesus' kingship, incense his divinity, myrrh his sacred humanity that was to experience death and burial.

As we contemplate this aspect of the nativity scene, we are called to reflect on the responsibility of every Christian to spread the Gospel. Each of us is called to

bear glad tidings to all, testifying by our practical works of mercy to the joy of knowing Jesus and his love.

The Magi teach us that people can come to Christ by a very long route. Men of wealth, sages from afar, a thirst for the infinite, they set out on the long and perilous journey that would lead them to Bethlehem (cf. Mt 2:1-12). Great joy comes over them in the presence of the Infant King. They are not scandalised by the poor surroundings, but immediately fall to their knees to worship him.

Kneeling before him, they understand that the God who with sovereign wisdom guides the course of the stars also guides the course of history, casting down the mighty and raising up the lowly.

Upon their return home, they would certainly have told others of this amazing encounter with the Messiah, thus initiating the spread of the Gospel among the nations.

10. Standing before the Christmas crèche, we are reminded of the time when we were children, eagerly waiting to set it up. These memories make us all the more conscious of the precious gift received from those who passed on the faith to us. At the same time, they remind us of our duty to share this same experience with our children and our grandchildren. It does not matter how the nativity scene is arranged: it can always be the same or it can change from year to year. What matters is that it speaks to our lives. Wherever it is, and

whatever form it takes, the Christmas crèche speaks to us of the love of God, the God who became a child in order to make us know how close he is to every man, woman and child, regardless of their condition.

Dear brothers and sisters, the Christmas crèche is part of the precious yet demanding process of passing on the faith. Beginning in childhood, and at every stage of our lives, it teaches us to contemplate Jesus, to experience God's love for us, to feel and believe that God is with us and that we are with him, his children, brothers and sisters all, thanks to that Child who is the Son of God and the Son of the Virgin Mary. And to realise that in that knowledge we find true happiness. Like Saint Francis, may we open our hearts to this simple grace, so that from our wonderment a humble prayer may arise: a prayer of thanksgiving to God, who wished to share with us his all, and thus never to leave us alone.

Given in Greccio, at the Shrine of the Nativity,
on 1 December in the year 2019,
the seventh of my Pontificate.

Notes

1. Cf. Thomas of Celano, *First Life*, 84; *Franciscan Sources*, 469.
2. Ibid., 85; *Franciscan Sources*, 469.
3. Ibid., 86; *Franciscan Sources*, 470.